I HATE FLORIDA STATE
303 Reasons Why You Should, Too

Crane Hill
PUBLISHERS
BIRMINGHAM, ALABAMA

I HATE FLORIDA STATE
303 Reasons Why You Should, Too

by Paul Finebaum

CRANE HILL
PUBLISHERS

Copyright 1995 by Paul Finebaum

All rights reserved
Printed in the United States of America
Published by Crane Hill Publishers

Library of Congress Cataloging-in-Publication Data

Finebaum, Paul 1955-
   I hate Florida State: 303 reasons why you should, too / by Paul Finebaum. — 1st ed.
      p.   cm.
   ISBN 1-881548-32-5
1. Florida State Seminoles (Football team) — Miscellanea. I. Title
GV958.F56F55   1995
796.323'63'0975988–dc20   95-34956
                                                                            CIP

10   9   8   7   6   5   4   3   2

I HATE FLORIDA STATE

I Hate Florida State Because…

1. Bobby Bowden once lost the Alabama job to Bill Curry, which is like coming home and finding out your wife ran off with Don Knotts.

2. The television show *My Three Sons* is based on Bowden and his family.

3. The FDA is considering allowing motivational speeches by Mickey Andrews to become legal replacements for sleeping pills.

4. The Florida State business school has a course called "Managing a 7–11."

5. Bowden is so cheap that he once took a free visit to Dr. Kevorkian.

6. Darrell Royal put it best when he said, "I know they bend the rules down there, but I was watching a game between Miami and FSU and they started the game with a burglar alarm."

7. FSU broadcaster Gene Deckerhoff has been spotted downtown wearing the sign "Will broadcast for food."

8. Vic Prinzi has one that says "Will do anything for food."

9. "How to Avoid Paying for Merchandise at Foot Locker" is a required course for scholarship football players.

10. FSU has a graduate course in how to avoid marrying your next of kin.

11. Aunt Bee was once captain of the FSU cheerleading squad.

12. Burt Reynolds is the biggest jerk to ever pass through FSU.

13. Or the state of Florida.

14. Or, for that matter, the entire universe.

15. Approximately 43% of FSU fans still have their front teeth.

16. Forrest Gump chose Alabama over FSU because he wanted an academic challenge.

17. FSU sorority girls are so stuck-up that they won't buy ladyfingers unless they're manicured.

18. The No. 1 cologne used by FSU players is Sportscreme.

19. Some FSU business majors think an asset is a little donkey.

20. Hootie Ingram once worked at FSU.

21. FSU has a graduate course in belching.

22. Seminole fans think the book *Beginning of Time* was about the day Bobby Bowden arrived in Tallahassee.

23. FSU spelled backward is USF, which is a much better school.

24. William Kennedy Smith teaches a summer school course at FSU called "How to Beat a Rape Charge."

25. The bestselling CD on the FSU campus is the background noise from Scott Bentley's last date.

26. FSU fans think "007" refers to the GPA of the Seminole football team.

27. Deion Sanders said he considered majoring in journalism at FSU because he was bored with basketweaving.

28. Corey Sawyer has written a new book titled *How to Hire the Right Agent.*

29. An academic All–American at FSU is someone who goes to class once a semester.

30. FSU chose to join the ACC over the SEC because the letters were easier for the football players to remember.

31. FSU fans talk about rebuilding after a 2–loss season.

32. Pat Kennedy believes that "Planet Reebok" is the planet right before Pluto.

33. Some FSU history professors claim the book *War and Peace* is about the relationship between Bobby Bowden and Steve Spurrier.

34. Bowden is so slow that he thinks Jenny Craig is a former homecoming queen.

35. Charlie Ward said the reason he didn't want to play for the CFL is that he didn't enjoy traveling overseas.

36. FSU graduates keep their diplomas in their rear windows so they can park in handicapped spaces.

37. Gennifer Flowers has a crush on Bobby Bowden.

38. FSU players wear Nike shoes on dates, hoping their girlfriends will say, "Just do it."

39. Some people think the book *The Client* is about Corey Sawyer.

40. Chuck Amato once said that the show *Little House on the Prairie* was about the first house on the Tallahassee campus.

41. Deion Sanders learned humility at FSU.

42. FSU basketball players can do almost everything with the ball but sign it.

43. FSU fans refuse to visit Mount Rushmore because Bobby Bowden's face isn't featured on it.

44. The reason Bowden doesn't get much mail is that only 13% of FSU fans can spell their name.

45. FSU basketball players believe a fast break is leaving a Foot Locker store without paying.

46. Bobby Bowden can say absolutely nothing and mean it.

47. You can always tell the most valuable player at FSU–he's the one with the most gold teeth.

48. Sandy D'Alemberte always has 2 seats in the FSU president's box–1 for himself and 1 for his ego.

49. FSU cheerleaders are tested weekly for makeup poisoning.

50. A favorite pickup line of FSU players is "Didn't we almost flunk out together?"

51. FSU football players are not required to go to the library before they graduate. However, they must learn how to spell it.

52. Bob Goin left FSU as athletic director to open a roof repair business.

53. If Wayne Hogan died during a football game, how would anyone know?

54. Doak Campbell's first name was really Dork.

55. Jeff Bowden has every book in the *Nancy Drew* series.

56. *The Odd Couple* was the real-life story of Bobby Bowden and Mickey Andrews.

57. FSU fans are taught in high school not to smoke at their own weddings.

58. Some FSU fans thought the movie *The Fugitive* was about Corey Sawyer.

59. FSU fans think Armageddon is if Florida ever beats the Seminoles in football.

60. The Zebras gave FSU the Orange Bowl victory over Nebraska.

61. Bobby Bowden talks about not being a quitter, but he quit the Alabama football team.

62. Had he stayed there, he probably would have replaced the Bear and had a career at a respectable school.

63. Deion Sanders had a hard time making enemies at FSU because his friends hated him so much.

64. FSU fans believe McDonald's is gourmet food.

65. FSU fans believe they should only drink liquids with names ending in "ade."

66. FSU fans think that The Golf Channel is more educational than C–Span.

67. Gene Deckerhoff can't talk and chew gum at the same time.

68. You can always tell when it's finals time in Tallahassee—that's when the football players buy their books.

69. Bobby Bowden has a Venus's-flytrap in his mouth—that's why it's always open.

70. Chief Osceola goes both ways.

71. Deion Sanders learned how to talk from Bobby Bowden.

72. FSU fans think Dr. Scholl's is the team doctor.

73. The Moore Athletic Center has a new smoke detector because the FSU cheerleaders' perfume kept setting off the old one.

74. FSU had not lost an ACC football game going into the 1995 season–like that is really a major accomplishment.

75. The top 10 biggest jerks to ever play for FSU are: Lee Corso.

76. Lee Corso.

77. Lee Corso.

78. Lee Corso.

79. Lee Corso.

80. Lee Corso.

81. Lee Corso.

82. Lee Corso.

83. Lee Corso.

84. Lee Corso.

85. FSU has a class for football players in how to turn on the dishwasher.

86. Mickey Andrews's favorite television show is *Bowling for Dollars*.

87. Tamarick Vanover has trouble spelling his own name.

88. Derrick Brooks was FSU's All-American nominee because he spelled his name correctly and got the date right.

89. FSU fans are getting sick of Burt Reynolds hanging around Tallahassee.

90. FSU fans wish Burt Reynolds would either get a real job or stop sponging off them.

91. The ESPN Saturday night game has played havoc with Seminole fans taking their weekly baths.

92. Bug zappers with Charlie Ward's picture on them are hot Christmas items this year.

93. Fred Biletnikoff learned everything he knows at FSU.

94. Ed Williamson was FSU's first big-time coach. He went 0-5 his first and last season.

95. Darrel Mudra used to coach the Seminoles from the press box. With a 4-18 record over 2 years, he was afraid to get near the fans.

96. FSU fans think the Civil War was fought between Miami and FSU.

97. In 1973 Larry Jones ended his 3 years at FSU in style. He lost to Florida 49–0, thus wrapping up a perfect 0–11 season.

98. Bobby Bowden wants to be buried in the "Sod Cemetery."

99. Some people wish they would bury his mouth there now.

100. When the FSU team went to the White House after the national championship, some of the players were so desperate that they tried to pick up Hillary.

101. However, Hillary spent most of the time flirting with Chief Osceola.

102. Sandy D'Alemberte once cracked a joke.

103. The rumor is that Ann Bowden once said to her husband, "You love football more than me." Bobby replied, "That is true, but I love you more than basketball."

104. Bowden is so cheap that he deducts charitable contributions to the widow of the Unknown Soldier.

105. The toughest thing that Deion Sanders ever tried to do at FSU was outtalk Bobby Bowden.

106. Bowden is such an optimist that he actually looked forward to getting married.

107. Tallahassee is such a small town that the picture postcards are blank.

108. Bobby Bowden used to be humble, but he broke himself of the habit.

109. FSU finally had the courage to beat Miami–it was the year they had almost as many players arrested as the Hurricanes did.

110. A poll of FSU fans revealed the 10 men they most wanted their sons to be like are: David Lamm.

111. Mike Tyson.

112. Corey Sawyer.

113. Gene Frenette.

114. John Nogoswski.

115. Ronald McDonald.

116. Kato Kaelin.

117. Howard Stern.

118. Wolf Blitzer.

119. Pee-wee Herman.

120. Bobby Bowden is so old that when he was a teenager, the Dead Sea was still alive.

121. Scott Bentley once said, "FSU football is great because you get to bite, kick, scratch, fight, and get sweaty–and afterward hug a blond."

122. Scott Bentley may not be much of a field goal kicker, but from the sound of things, he has some pretty good moves.

123. The tape of Bentley and a friend proved that he doesn't always choke under pressure.

124. David Lamm's favorite drink is Rolaids and Perrier.

125. The hotels are so bad near the FSU campus that to get room service you have to dial 911.

126. Mickey Andrews is so dense that he looks for a wishbone in a soft-boiled egg.

127. FSU shortened its nickname to "Noles" to give some of the defensive players a better shot at spelling it correctly.

128. Deion Sanders once said, "If we didn't have to go to class, this really would be a cool school."

129. Sandy D'Alemberte once dated Marcia Clark.

130. Forrest Gump wanted to go to FSU until he found out that it was in Tallahassee.

131. Anyone at FSU who subscribes to *The Wall Street Journal* is considered a genius.

132. Bobby Bowden can say less in more time than any human being in the world.

133. Only in Bowden's offense can a player like Charlie Ward win the Heisman and not find a job in the NFL.

134. After losing to Miami Bowden said, "I now know why we lost the Civil War—we must have had the same officials."

135. Bowden once called Dr. Kevorkian collect after a loss to Miami.

136. FSU graduates get lifetime memberships in Tupperware clubs.

137. The top 10 favorite things to do after an FSU homecoming game are: Listen to Scott Bentley's mood tapes.

138. Take a Saturday night bath.

139. Sleep in until 5 a.m.

140. Go to Hardee's and watch them make steak and biscuits.

141. Look at the lingerie section in the JC Penney catalog.

142. Give blood at the Red Cross to help pay for tuition.

143. Beat a Steve Spurrier blow-up doll.

144. Watch reruns of *Bonanza*.

145. Drive down to the police station and get autographs of FSU players on their way to a lineup.

146. Go to Kmart early for the Blue Light Special.

147. Some of the sportswriters who voted FSU No. 1 over Notre Dame after the 1994 Orange Bowl aren't qualified to vote in the *People's Choice Awards.*

148. Bowden cried so much about No. 1 that the voters felt sorry for him.

149. Bowden should have been given a cookie and a glass of milk instead of a national championship ring.

150. FSU has a graduate class in how to change the oil in your car.

151. During freshman orientation, the school has a course in how to brush your teeth.

152. Counting to 500 is a requirement for the Ph.D. program at FSU.

153. Making spitballs is a favorite pastime of FSU football players.

154. Delta Burke came in second for homecoming queen.

155. She actually won, but after she broke the scale, the officials took away her crown.

156. The 8 words guaranteed to break any FSU cheerleader's heart are "Sorry, honey, we just ran out of bacon."

157. Sandy D'Alemberte's first name is actually Talbot.

158. A romantic date for an FSU coed is going to the Shoney's breakfast bar.

159. Bowling alleys in Tallahassee have forbidden scratching between frames.

160. Football players at FSU must pass the course "How to Walk Your Dog" before getting their degree.

161. Last year's homecoming queen was so ugly that when they took her to the top of FSU's tallest building, she was attacked by a plane.

162. After reading Bobby Bowden's autobiography, one critic wrote, "Once you put it down, you can't pick it up again."

163. Mickey Andrews is so dull that he lights up a room when he leaves it.

164. There is something to be said for Bobby Bowden—and he is usually saying it.

165. The FSU campus doesn't need a Comedy Club. All the students need to do for a laugh is look at FSU's conference schedule in the ACC.

166. Bobby Bowden once said before a Miami game, "Gentlemen, you are going to whip Miami or I'm going to whip you."

167. After trailing at the half, Bowden is reputed to have said, "If we lose, I'll still love you and your mommas will still love you, but I can't make any promises about your girlfriends."

168. Joey Buttafuoco has never missed an FSU–Miami game.

169. Scott Bentley never met a taperecorder he didn't like.

170. FSU considered joining the SEC a few years back but was afraid of a dirty word—competition.

171. When Bentley was asked which record he treasured most at FSU, he responded, "I think it was *Hotel California* by the Eagles."

172. Deion Sanders still believes that he is a distant relative of Colonel Sanders.

173. Sanders changed his nickname from "Neon Deion" to "Prime Time" because it was easier to spell.

174. Pat Kennedy promised to turn the FSU program around quickly. He has done so by taking the school from the NCAA to oblivion in a short time.

175. It was no surprise that Tallahassee voted Republican in the last election considering how many key FSU field goals went right.

176. Charlie Ward made the basketball team at FSU because anybody could.

177. The only thing that could make the FSU players happier than winning the national championship is if they made shoplifting legal.

178. Before the 1994 regular season game between Florida and FSU, Bowden gave a "Tie one for the Gipper" speech.

179. With that kind of attitude, one must hope Bowden never becomes an army general.

180. If tying a game is like kissing your sister, one must assume Bowden's sister looks like Julia Roberts.

181. The best thing about Bobby Bowden's retirement is that perhaps Burt Reynolds will quit hanging around FSU games.

182. Burt Reynolds's hairpiece is older than Chief Osceola.

183. Most people would rather barf than listen to the FSU war chant.

184. Does anyone know how Talbot "Sandy" D'Alemberte got his nickname?

185. The movie *The Day the World Ended* is about FSU's annual game with Miami.

186. Caning must be legal in Miami because the Seminoles get beaten every year they visit.

187. FSU fans think that a pair of Dockers is a couple of longshoremen.

188. Some fans don't understand why they go to a dentist to get a crown and don't leave with one on their head.

189. Other fans believe that a bong is not an instrument for drug use, but the sound of 2 FSU quarterbacks colliding.

190. FSU fans think that a honeymoon is when 2 lovers bare their buttocks toward a public building.

191. Mickey Andrews still can't understand that the sorority Phi Mu is not some place where cows graze.

192. Danny Kannel thinks that a racist is someone who drives on the NASCAR circuit.

193. Charlie Ward once said, "A mind is a terrible thing to waste so I am donating mine to FSU."

194. Some FSU fans think that a jockstrap is a football player who's into S&M.

195. Some fans of FSU take their kids to McDonald's and actually look for the farm.

196. A number of FSU players think that the leading rusher each year is the president of the sorority with the biggest pledge class.

197. Players think "higher education" is when students have classes on the top floor of Dirac Library.

198. Bobby Bowden goes to Floyd the Barber for his monthly trim.

199. Some fans believe the "Big Ten" refers to the top 10 finalists in the Miss FSU contest.

200. Some FSU graduates believe the Gulf War was fought in Destin.

201. Mickey Andrews once cracked open a bottle of champagne when he received a letter from Publisher's Clearing House saying he was a finalist for a million bucks.

202. Asked about manual labor in an economics class, Charlie Ward answered, "He was a great Mexican leader."

203. A number of FSU fans are convinced that Steve Spurrier is related to Saddam Hussein.

204. Bobby Bowden declared a national day of celebration when Dennis Erickson resigned at Miami.

205. John Hinckley is an FSU fan.

206. Hinckley's favorite pastime, other than dreaming of Jodie Foster, is listening to old tapes of Vic Prinzi.

207. FSU teaches that a playboy is just another word for FSU's kicker, Scott Bentley.

208. Alumni think that a Rhodes Scholar is a student traveling down Pensacola Street.

209. Some followers of FSU football think that a Winnebago is a luxury car.

210. The FDA is considering allowing the recording of the Pat Kennedy television show to be used in place of sleeping pills.

211. Sandy D'Alemberte fell in love with himself as a teenager. That way, he figured he wouldn't have any rivals.

212. Bobby Bowden's favorite kind of party is whine and cheese.

213. Outside Moore Athletic Center there's a sign that reads "Bein' an idiot is no box of chocolates."

214. The 3 hardest words in the English language for an FSU fan to say are "I was wrong."

215. The top 10 things to do on a Saturday night in the off-season in Tallahassee are: Watch the replay of the 1994 Orange Bowl against Nebraska.

216. Watch a replay of the 1995 Sugar Bowl against Florida.

217. Watch the final episode of *Get Smart*.

218. Clean the family jewels.

219. Beat the wife.

220. Beat the dog.

221. Beat the dog's wife.

222. Beat the wife's dog.

223. Study for driver's test.

224. Clean the outhouse.

225. Red Man outsells toilet paper at local 7–11 stores.

226. FSU football players get their early morning workouts by fighting for the toy in the Lucky Charms box.

227. Bobby Bowden once devoured an entire Shoney's breakfast bar by himself.

228. FSU has a new course called "How to Install a Screen-Saver on Your Computer."

229. The car of choice for FSU football players is a white Ford Bronco.

230. The tattoo shop in Tallahassee is the busiest place in town on Saturday mornings.

231. The only difference between Deion Sanders and Mr. T. is Mr. T. wears less jewelry.

232. Mickey Andrews is next on a waiting list for a charisma bypass.

233. Al Cowlings will be guest of honor next year at the FSU spring game.

234. Anthropologists have asked to see X-rays of Bobby Bowden's skull for display at the National Museum.

235. FSU fraternities require pledges to walk and chew gum at the same time before initiation.

236. Before declaring a major, freshmen at FSU are required to declare their favorite dancing raisin.

237. The most popular drug in Tallahassee is Geritol.

238. Sandy D'Alemberte is such an egomanic that he often gets upset at funerals because he's not the corpse.

239. FSU is the only school in the state where the toilets have 3 different languages written on the walls.

240. Bobby Bowden's top 10 favorite diet foods are: Chicken-fried steak.

241. Lightly fried onion rings.

242. Gently-fried egg rolls.

243. Stuckey's low-fat pecan log.

244. Stuckey's low-fat caramel brownies.

245. Goo-Goo Clusters with artificial sweetener.

246. Low-fat Vienna sausage.

247. Big Macs without the special sauce, cheese, and pickles.

248. French-fried cucumber sandwich.

249. Cheeseburger without the cheese.

250. The captain of the FSU cheerleading squad has a 40-inch bust and an IQ to match.

251. Bowden's waistline has expanded more quickly than the national debt.

252. The part of Bowden that has really expanded is his mouth–which is already past the legal limit.

253. The FSU coaching staff had to start separating Wives' Day and Girlfriends' Day because a couple of guys brought both.

254. One of the top selling videos in Tallahassee is of the Miami riots.

255. Listening to Gene Deckerhoff is the latest cure for insomnia in the Florida Panhandle.

256. If Bowden ever writes another book, a good idea for a title would be *All the Different Ways I've Blown the Miami Game.*

257. In 1991, FSU went from No. 1 in the country to No. 3 in the state in a span of 3 glorious weeks.

258. Brad Scott was one of the smartest coaches to ever work on Bowden's staff–he left.

259. Danny Kannel honestly believes that the Panama Canal was named after him.

260. FSU freshmen recently voted *The Price Is Right* as their favorite show because it reminds them so much of their recruitment.

261. *Let's Make a Deal* finished second.

262. It is hard to tell the difference between a Barbie doll and an FSU cheerleader.

263. Except a Barbie doll has more personality.

264. And Barbie dolls are less plastic.

265. Mickey Andrews has a pinup of Fred Flintstone in his office.

266. FSU's communications school has a class in hosting segments of the Consumer Shopping Network.

267. Some FSU students believe the book *How the Grinch Stole Christmas* is about the Miami–FSU series.

268. The FSU homecoming queen was so ugly that she wore a turtleneck to cover her flea collar.

269. When Bowden is ill, he doesn't need X-rays—everybody can see right through him.

270. Bowden's mouth is so big that he can whisper in his own ear.

271. Bowden has gotten so old that his mind has gone from passion to pension.

272. Chief Osceola has obviously never heard the word "deodorant."

273. Some FSU coaches originally thought that Charlie Ward was a place where former Vietnam vets were housed.

274. Deion Sanders was always upset that Burt Reynolds dated Renegade before he could make a move.

275. The video of the 1989 FSU–Southern Miss game is not a big seller at the campus bookstore.

276. FSU's first bowl game was the 1949 Cigar Bowl against Wofford.

277. Lee Corso is to FSU football what Barney Fife is to law enforcement.

278. Burt Reynolds's first acting job at FSU was being the understudy for Chief Osceola.

279. Scott Bentley has the only apartment in Tallahassee equipped with an instant replay camera.

280. For years Gene Deckerhoff was an unknown failure–now he is a known failure.

281. David Lamm has no prejudices–he hates everyone equally.

282. Some FSU fans think the movie *Grumpy Old Men* is about Bobby Bowden and Mickey Andrews.

283. FSU cheerleaders only like sex on days that have a "d" in them.

284. Scott Bentley has a sign on the door to his bedroom that reads "Are you live or on tape?"

285. Bobby Bowden recently ran into someone he knew when they were the same age.

286. The bestselling book in the FSU campus store this winter will be *I Hate Paul Finebaum*.

287. The No. 2 book will be *I Hate Miami.*

288. The No. 3 book will be *I Hate Florida.*

289. If Lee Corso and Bowden went out to dinner, they could talk each other to death.

290. One of Bobby Bowden's favorite fantasies as a kid was being in a one-act play.

291. His favorite fantasy today is Miami shutting down its football program.

292. His second is beating his son Terry in a game.

293. Tallahassee isn't the end of the world, but you can sure see it from there.

294. Bowden's best joke ever is his record against Miami.

295. Of all the songs ever recorded, the one Bowden hates the most is Simon & Garfunkel's "Sounds of Silence."

296. No. 2 is Scott Bentley's greatest hit.

297. The only time Bobby Bowden is ever speechless is when someone asks him the last time he skipped a meal.

298. When Wayne Hogan's doctor told him recently to eat more vegetables, he started putting 2 olives in every martini.

299. Mickey Andrews is the kind of guy who goes to an orgy and complains about the cheese dip.

300. Sandy D'Alemberte is so dull that when he goes to vote, they hand him an absentee ballot.

301. Bobby Bowden once told Ann, "I love you terribly." She said, "You sure do."

302. Asked once how his wife felt about his 18-hour days at FSU, Bobby Bowden replied, "I don't know—I don't see her that much."

303. Ann Bowden was once asked the secret of her marriage to Bobby. She said, "We take time to go to a restaurant two times a week. A little candlight dinner, soft music, and dancing. He goes Tuesdays— I go Fridays."